# SSAT QUICK

Welcome, students and parent~ ~ ~ ~ ~ give you a quick review of the most essential content, strategies, and tips for the SSAT. For comprehensive prep, Ivy Global also offers a full set of SSAT books: *SSAT English, SSAT Math,* and *SSAT Practice*. These products are available for purchase at ssatprep.com or amazon.com.

# ABOUT THE PUBLISHER

This publication was edited by the team at Ivy Global. Ivy Global is a pioneering education company that delivers a wide range of educational services. The SSAT content was adapted from the material in our SSAT Book Series.

Editors: Sacha Azor, Stephanie Bucklin, and Nicole Young
Producers: Lloyd Min and Junho Suh

Proofreaders: Alexandra Candib, Shavumiyaa Chandrabalan, Natalia Cole, Laurel Durning-Hammond, Lei Huang, Gideon Ng, Yolanda Song, Adam Wolsky, and Camille Wong

E-mail: publishing@ivyglobal.com
Website: http://www.ivyglobal.com

# About The SSAT

The SSAT consists of three main sections (Verbal, Math, and Reading), plus a Writing Sample that either takes the form of a creative writing assignment or an essay. The format of the test differs based on the level of the exam:

| Elementary Level | | |
|---|---|---|
| Section | Questions | Length |
| Math | 30 questions | 30 min |
| Verbal | 30 questions | 20 min |
| Reading | 28 questions | 30 min |
| Writing | One prompt | 15 min |

| Middle and Upper Levels | | |
|---|---|---|
| Section | Questions | Length |
| Writing | One prompt | 25 min |
| Math I | 25 questions | 30 min |
| Reading | 40 questions | 40 min |
| Verbal | 60 questions | 30 min |
| Math II | 25 questions | 30 min |
| Experimental Section | 16 questions | 15 min |

Except for the Writing Sample, all questions are **multiple choice** (A) to (E). You are not allowed to use calculators, rulers, dictionaries, or other aids during the exam.

# TEST DAY CHECKLIST

- ☐ Photo Admission Ticket
- ☐ Approved Photo ID
- ☐ No. 2 pencils and erasers
- ☐ A watch
- ☐ Snack and water bottle
- ☐ I have directions to the test center and I have instructions for finding the entrance.
- ☐ I am leaving at _____ a.m. on test day. This allows time for delays.
- ☐ I have set my alarm.

You need to be on time, or you can't take the test!

# GRIDDING ANSWER CHOICES

For the Middle and Upper Level exams, you must enter your answers on a separate answer sheet. Keep your answer sheet neat and avoid stray marks. Below, Answer 6 shows the correct way to input your answers:

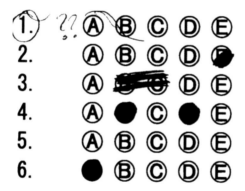

# IMPORTANT STRATEGIES

## SCORING

- 1 mark is awarded for every question answered correctly.
- ¼ mark is deducted for every question answered incorrectly.
- No marks are awarded or deducted for questions left blank.

## STRATEGIES

1. Grid your answer choices correctly and carefully.
   a. **Circle your answer choice in your test booklet** so you can easily check your circled answers against your gridded ones if you have time.
   b. **Create a system for marking questions that you skipped.** For example, draw a star or a question mark next to the question in the booklet.
   c. **Grid your answers in batches of four, five, or six answer choices.** That way, you do not have to go back and forth between your test booklet and your answer sheet for every question.
2. Pace yourself to manage your time effectively.
   a. **Skip those questions you are uncertain of** unless you can eliminate one or more answer choices.
3. Learn a strategic approach for multiple-choice questions.
   a. **Make predictions.** Try to come up with an answer on your own before looking at the answer choices.
   b. **Use Process of Elimination.** To narrow down your answer choices, think about the potential incorrect answers and actively identify those to eliminate them.
   c. **Try back-solving.** For some math problems, you may be able to plug in and test answer choices to find the correct solution.

# WRITING STRUCTURE / TIPS

## BUDGET YOUR TIME

Plan to spend no more than a few minutes choosing your prompt, brainstorming, and planning, and save a few minutes at the end to edit.

## QUICK WRITING TIPS

- Use the author's full name the first time you use it (you can just use his or her last name after).
- Avoid using phrases like "a lot" and "really."
- Avoid the passive voice—Ex: Write "Joe wrote the essay" (active voice) instead of "The essay was written by Joe" (passive voice).
- Avoid run-on sentences.

## THE SHORT STORY: ALL LEVELS

- Establish a character and setting.
- One conflict is usually sufficient.
- Pay attention to the tense (past or present) and point of view (first person or third person) used in the prompt, and use the same ones in your story.
- Show, don't tell.
- Make use of figurative language like similes, metaphors, and personification, if appropriate.
- Use dialogue tags effectively, and start a new paragraph each time the speaker changes.
- Give your story a beginning, middle, and end.

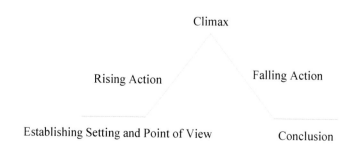

Climax

Rising Action

Falling Action

Establishing Setting and Point of View

Conclusion

# THE ESSAY: UPPER LEVEL ONLY

## PERSUASIVE WRITING

Requires you to take a side on an issue:

- (Introduction) Clearly state your position (your thesis statement), which your entire essay will support.
- (2-3 body paragraphs) Use concrete examples to support your position.
    - History, science, literature, or current events examples work best.
    - Well-described personal examples can also be effective.
    - Be as specific as possible.
- (Conclusion) Conclude your essay by refuting (disproving) a counterargument and restating your thesis.

## INFORMATIVE WRITING

Aims to describe, define, explain, inform, or show cause and effect. Two main types:

1. A **descriptive essay**: requires you to describe or define characteristics or qualities.

    Tips: Stick to topics you know. Choose two or three qualities you'd like to discuss and explain how they relate to your subject.

2. A **cause and effect essay**: requires you to describe a situation and analyze its possible causes and effects.

    Tips: Identify causes, explain effects, and offer solutions. Explain how things can be done differently to improve the situation. Narrate possibilities and show potential outcomes.

# VERBAL REVIEW / REFERENCE

## SYNONYM STRATEGIES

- Start by covering up the answer choices and thinking of your own definition for the word in capital letters.
- Come up with **contexts**—phrases where you might have heard the word before. A word's context is everything in a phrase or sentence that might influence the word's meaning.
- Think of the word's **connotation**—its secondary meaning, or the feeling we get from the word. A word can have a positive connotation if it means something good, a negative connotation if it means something bad, or a neutral connotation if it is neither good nor bad.

## ANALOGY STRATEGIES

- Create a **connector** to describe the relationship between the words. (Ex: Cow is to calf → A cow is the mother of a calf)
- Be as specific as possible.
- Read your connector in the same order for both the question and the answers.

### TYPES OF ANALOGIES

1. **Synonym and Antonym Analogies**: Some of the most basic word relationships are **synonyms** (words that mean the same thing) and **antonyms** (words that have opposite or contrasting meanings).

   Ex: Adoring is to loving as amazement is to awe. (*Synonym*)

   Ex: Hope is to despair as empty is to full. (*Antonym*)

2. **Intensity and Degree Analogies**: Sometimes words can be synonyms, but differ in **intensity** or **degree**.

   Ex: Hungry is to starving as unkind is to vicious.

3. **Part and Whole Analogies**: You may have to decide whether both words are part of the same whole, or whether one word is a part and the other word is a whole.

   Ex: Player is to team as actor is to cast.

4. **Examples and Types**: Sometimes a word is not necessarily a part of a group, but an **example** or **type** of a larger category.

   Ex: Hound is to dog as influenza is to virus.

5. **Use and Function Analogies**: **Use** and **function** analogies name two objects connected by their function, or one object and another word describing how or by whom it is used.

   Ex: Pencil is to write as brush is to paint.

LESS COMMON TYPES OF ANALOGIES

6. **Location Analogies**: places or nationalities that are connected by location.

   Ex: Germany is to Europe as Kenya is to Africa.

7. **Spelling or Rhyming Analogies**: not connected by meaning, but by the order of their letters.

   Ex: Tar is to rat as bur is to rub.

8. **Vertical Analogies**: ask you to create a relationship (connector) between *one word in the question and one word in the answer*, rather than between the two words in the question.

   Ex: Dog is to cat as canine is to feline.

### If You Get Stuck

- If you don't know a word, try using your knowledge of **context** to guess at a relationship.
- Remember that you are looking for the **best fit**, which may be an answer choice with an unfamiliar word.

### What If You Can't Write A Connector?

- First check whether the question is a **vertical** analogy or a **spelling/rhyming** analogy. These two uncommon analogy types don't always make sense with a typical connector.
- If this doesn't work, look at the **types of words** being used in the question (noun, verb, adjective, adverb). If you're able to identify the types of words in an analogy question, the correct answer choice will most likely have the same types of words.

# READING REVIEW / REFERENCE

## TIPS

- Focus on the shorter passages first and save the long passages for last.
- Read quickly: try to understand the main points rather than the small details. Don't waste time trying to understand every piece of information.
- Answer questions about the main idea or the main purpose first, and then turn to questions that ask about specific details in the passage.
- Underline the **key words** and **transitional words**.
- Try to guess the meaning of unfamiliar words **in context**, by looking for clues nearby in the sentence.

## TYPES OF PASSAGES

1. Informative passages: explain or describe a main topic. (Ex: articles in an encyclopedia, textbook, or even a newspaper)
2. Persuasive passages: convince the reader of a specific position or argument. (Ex: political speech, opinion essay, newspaper op-ed)
   a. Try to imagine who is speaking and who his or her intended audience might be.
   b. Pay close attention to the author's **tone**. Because a persuasive passage presents an opinion, the author will frequently have a **positive** or **negative** feeling about the topic he or she is discussing.
3. Short stories: fiction
   a. Figure out if the story is from the **first-person point of view** or the **third-person point of view**.
   b. The **theme** of a story is its "main idea," or the message it conveys about life and behavior.
4. Poetry: expresses an idea through highly imaginative language.
   a. Main Components: lines, stanzas, meter (rhythm of stressed and unstressed syllables), rhyme.
   b. Figurative Language: imagery, symbolism, simile, metaphor, personification.

## TYPES OF QUESTIONS

1.  Main idea questions: ask about the author's main topic, theme, or thesis.

    a.  Pay close attention to the first and last sentences of the passage, because they frequently give you information about its main idea.

    b.  Eliminate answer options that are **too broad** or **too specific**.

2.  Specific detail questions: ask you to summarize or interpret specific information mentioned in the passage.

    a.  Always **go back to the passage** to see where you might find the information you need.

    b.  Pay close attention to the words **NOT**, **LEAST**, and **EXCEPT** in the questions.

    c.  **Roman numeral questions** (I, II, and III) ask you to check multiple pieces of information in the passage. Check to see whether each of the Roman numeral statements is true.

    d.  **Vocabulary in context questions** feature words that often have multiple possible definitions. Plug the answer choices back into the original sentence to make sure you have picked the author's definition.

3.  Genre and tone questions: ask you to analyze how the author is writing.

    a.  **Genre**: the type of passage—informative, persuasive passage, short story, or poem.

    b.  **Tone**: the author's attitude toward the topic—neutral, emotionally involved, etc.

4.  Inference questions: ask you to make a logical guess or assumption based on the information in the passage—analyzing what is implied but not directly stated.

    a.  Pick an answer choice that best matches the author's primary purpose in the passage.

    b.  If the question is asking you to guess **what might happen next** in the passage, think about the author's purpose and main point. Then, think about what other information could be included to continue expanding upon this main point.

    c.  Pay particular attention to images and metaphors in poetry. These often have many levels of meaning beyond the literal surface reading.

# Common Word Roots, Prefixes, and Suffixes

| Common Roots | | |
|---|---|---|
| Root | Meaning | Examples |
| ag, act | do | action, agent |
| ami, amo | love | amiable, amorous |
| anim | mind, soul, spirit | animal, animate, unanimous |
| aud, audit | hear | audible, auditorium, audience |
| auto | self | autobiography, autograph |
| ben | good | beneficial, benevolence |
| bio | life | biography, biology |
| carn | flesh, meat | carnivore, carnal, incarnate |
| chron | time | chronology, synchronize |
| civi | citizen | civilization, civilian, civil |
| corp | body | corporation, corporeal, corpse |
| cid, cis | cut, kill | incision, homicide, insecticide |
| dic, dict | speak | dictate, contradict |
| domin | master | dominant, domain, domineering |
| err | wander | error, erratic, errand |
| eu | good, beautiful | euphoria, euphemism |
| fall, fals | deceive | fallacious, infallible, falsify |
| fid | faith | fidelity, confide, confidence |
| graph, gram | writing | grammar, telegraph |
| loqu, locut | talk | soliloquy, loquacious |
| luc | light | elucidate, lucid, translucent |
| magn | great | magnify, magnate, magnanimous |
| mal | bad | malevolent, malicious |
| mori, mort | die | mortuary, immortal, moribund |
| nom | name | misnomer, nominal |
| nov | new | novice, innovate, renovate, novelty |
| omni | all | omniscient, omnipotent |
| pac, pas, pax | peace | pacify, pacific, pacifist, passive |
| phil | love | philanthropist, philosophy |
| port | carry | portable, porter, transport, export |
| poten | able, powerful | potential, omnipotent, impotent |

| reg, rect | rule | regicide, regime, regent, insurrection |
|---|---|---|
| sacr, secr | holy | sacred, sacrilegious, consecrate |
| scribe, script | write | describe, script |
| spec, spic | see, look | spectators, retrospect |
| tang, tact, ting | touch | tactile, tangent, contact |
| terr | land | terrain, terrestrial, subterranean |
| urb | city | urban, urbane, suburban |
| vac | empty | vacation, evacuate, vacant |
| ver | truth | veracity, verify, veracious |
| viv, vit | alive | revival, vivacious, vitality |

| Common Prefixes | | |
|---|---|---|
| Prefix | Meaning | Examples |
| ambi, amphi | both | ambiguous, ambivalent |
| an, a | without | anarchy, amoral |
| anti | against | antipathy, antisocial |
| circum | around | circumspect, circumscribe |
| co, col, com, con | with, together | coauthor, collaborate, composition |
| contra, contro | against | contradict, contravene, controversy |
| di, dif, dis | not, apart | digress, differ, disparity |
| dys | abnormal, bad | dysfunction, dyslexia, dystopia |
| e, ex, extra, extro | out, beyond | expel, extrovert, eject |
| in, il, im, ir (1) | not | inefficient, illegible, irrepressible |
| in, il, im, ir (2) | in, upon | invite, illuminate, impression |
| inter | between, among | intervene, interjection |
| intra | within | intramural, intravenous |
| mis | bad, hatred | misdemeanor, misanthrope |
| mono | one | monarchy, monologue |
| non | not, without | nonentity, nondescript |
| pan | all, every | panacea, panorama, pandemic |
| poly | many | polygon, polygamist, polyglot |
| post | after | postpone, posterity |
| pre | before | preamble, premonition |
| pro | forward, for, before | propulsive, prologue |

| *re, retro* | again, back | reiterate, retrogress |
|---|---|---|
| *sub, suc, sup, sus* | under, less | subjugate, suppress |
| *super, sur* | over, above | superior, surtax |
| *syn, sym, syl, sys* | with, together | symmetry, synthesize, sympathize |
| *trans* | across | transfer, transpose |
| *un* | not | unabridged, unkempt |

| Common Suffixes | | |
|---|---|---|
| Suffix | Meaning | Examples |
| *able, ible* | ADJ: capable of | edible, presentable |
| *ac, ic, ical* | ADJ: like, related | cardiac, mythic, dramatic, musical |
| *acious, icious* | ADJ: full of | malicious, audacious |
| *ant, ent* | ADJ/N: full of | eloquent, verdant |
| *ate* | V: make, become | consecrate, eradicate |
| *en* | V: make, become | awaken, strengthen, soften |
| *er (1)* | ADJ: more | wiser, happier |
| *er (2)* | N: a person who does | teacher, baker |
| *cy, ty, ity* | N: state of being | democracy, veracity |
| *ful* | ADJ: full of | respectful, cheerful, wonderful |
| *fy* | V: to make | magnify, petrify, beautify |
| *ism* | N: doctrine, belief | monotheism, fanaticism, egoism |
| *ist* | N: dealer, doer | fascist, realist, artist |
| *ize, ise* | V: make | victimize, rationalize, harmonize |
| *logy* | N: study of | biology, geology, neurology |
| *oid* | ADJ: similar to | humanoid, anthropoid, spheroid |
| *ose/ous* | ADJ: full of | lachrymose, nauseous |
| *osis* | N: condition | psychosis, neurosis, hypnosis |
| *tion, sion* | N: state of being | exasperation, irritation |
| *tude* | N: state of | fortitude, certitude |

# MATH REVIEW

## TIPS

- Write down your work on the scratch paper provided.
- Break complicated problems into steps and tackle one step at a time.
- Use figures and diagrams provided (though note they are not necessarily drawn to scale unless the question says otherwise), or draw your own figure to help you organize your thoughts and information.
- Check your work.

## STRATEGIES

- **Guess and check**: Especially with **geometry** problems or problems where a diagram is given, you can narrow your choices down to one based on what seems reasonable, or try rounding to come to an approximate answer.
- **Picking numbers**: For **algebra** questions that contain a lot of variables, you can often pick an easy number to work with and plug this into the equation.
- **Back-solving**: Work backwards from the multiple-choice answers you are given. Only use back-solving if the answer choices don't include variables.
  - Hint: answer choices that are numbers are often given in order (smallest to largest, or largest to smallest). Start by plugging in the middle answer. If it doesn't work, you can determine whether to try a larger or smaller answer.

| Arithmetic Review | | |
|---|---|---|
| Name | Definition | Examples |
| **Integer** | any positive or negative whole number | -3, 1, 200 |
| **Operation** | a process that changes one number into another | $+, \ -, \ \times, \ \div$ |
| **Even Number** | divisible by 2 | 2, 4, 6, 8... |
| **Odd Number** | not divisible by 2 | 1, 3, 5, 7... |
| **Factor** | a number that another number is evenly divisible by | 3 is a factor of 12 |
| **Multiple** | a number that can be divided evenly by the original | 12 is a multiple of 3 |

| | | |
|---|---|---|
| **Prime Number** | has only 2 factors: 1 and itself | 2, 3, 5, 7, 11, 13, 17... |
| **Composite Number** | has more than 2 factors | 4, 6, 9, 10, 12, 15... |
| **Prime Factors** | prime numbers that, when multiplied, give the original number | 3, 3, and 2 for 12 |
| **Greatest Common Factor (GCF)** | largest integer that is a factor of both given integers | 8 is the GCF of 16 and 24 |
| **Least Common Multiple (LCM)** | smallest integer that is a multiple of both given integers | 48 is the LCM of 16 and 24 |
| **Patterns** | lists that follow a rule | |
| **Sequence** | a pattern involving numbers (called terms) | 5, 7, 9, 11, 13... or 5, 10, 20, 40, 80... |
| **Positive Numbers** | greater than zero | 1, 2, 3, 4, 5... |
| **Negative Numbers** | less than zero; negative sign in front | -1, -2, -3, -4, -5... |

*For more information, refer to the Ivy Global SSAT Math Guide (see pages 49-74).*

## FRACTIONS, RATIOS, DECIMALS, AND PERCENTS

| Converting Between Fractions, Decimals, and Percents | | |
|---|---|---|
| **Operation** | **Explanation** | **Example** |
| **Fraction → Decimal** | divide the numerator by the denominator using long division. | $\frac{1}{4} = 0.25$ |
| **Fraction → Percent** | convert the fraction into a decimal using long division, then multiply by 100%. | $\frac{1}{4} = 25\%$ |
| **Decimal → Fraction** | rewrite your decimal as a fraction with a denominator of 10, 100, or 1000 (depending how many digits are after the dot) and simplify. | $0.4 = \frac{4}{10} = \frac{2}{5}$ |
| **Decimal → Percent** | multiply by 100 and add a % sign. | $0.4 = 40\%$ |
| **Percent → Fraction** | put percent as the numerator and 100 as the denominator and simplify. | $35\% = \frac{35}{100} = \frac{7}{20}$ |
| **Percent → Decimal** | divide by 100 and remove % sign. | $35\% = 0.35$ |

# CONVERTING BETWEEN RATIOS AND FRACTIONS

A **ratio** represents a relationship between 2 or more parts. Both numbers in a ratio make up the whole. If a ratio of one part to another part is expressed in a fraction, you can write another fraction expressing one part to the whole by adding the numerator and the denominator of the original fraction and making it the denominator of your new fraction.

Ex: The ratio of boys to girls in a class is $\frac{2}{3}$. What is the fraction of boys in the class?

$$\frac{2}{2+3} = \frac{2}{5}$$

| Fractions | | |
|---|---|---|
| Category | Description | Examples |
| **Mixed Number** | combination of a whole number and a fraction | $3\frac{1}{2}$ |
| **Improper Fraction** | fraction where the numerator is bigger than the denominator | $\frac{11}{5}$ |
| **Adding and Subtracting Fractions** | convert fractions into equivalents (same denominator) and perform operations on numerator | $\frac{1}{7} + \frac{2}{7} = \frac{3}{7}$ |
| **Multiplying Fractions** | multiply the numerators and denominators separately | $\frac{1}{4} \times \frac{3}{5} = \frac{3}{20}$ |
| **Dividing Fractions** | multiply by the reciprocal of the second fraction | $\frac{1}{4} \div \frac{3}{5} = \frac{1}{4} \times \frac{5}{3} = \frac{5}{12}$ |
| **Cross-Multiplying** | If $\frac{a}{b} = \frac{c}{d}$ then $a \times d = c \times b$ | $\frac{3}{5} = \frac{6}{10}$ <br> $3 \times 10 = 6 \times 5$ |

*For more information, refer to the Ivy Global SSAT Math Guide (see pages 75-99).*

| Exponent Rules | |
|---|---|
| Rule | Example |
| $a^1 = a$ | $8^1 = 8$ |
| $a^0 = 1$ | $8^0 = 1$ |
| $a^{-m} = \frac{1}{a^m}$ | $8^{-2} = \frac{1}{8^2} = \frac{1}{64}$ |

| | |
|---|---|
| $a^{\frac{1}{m}} = \sqrt[m]{a}$ | $8^{\frac{1}{3}} = \sqrt[3]{8} = 2$ |
| $a^m a^n = a^{m+n}$ | $8^2 \times 8^3 = 8^{2+3} = 8^5 = 32768$ |
| $\dfrac{a^m}{a^n} = a^{m-n}$ | $\dfrac{8^3}{8^2} = 8^{3-2} = 8^1 = 8$ |
| $(a^m)^n = a^{mn}$ | $(8^2)^3 = 8^{2 \times 3} = 8^6 = 262144$ |
| $a^m b^m = (ab)^m$ | $8^3 \times 2^3 = (8 \times 2)^3 = 16^3 = 4096$ |
| $\dfrac{a^m}{b^m} = \left(\dfrac{a}{b}\right)^m$ | $\dfrac{8^3}{2^3} = \left(\dfrac{8}{2}\right)^3 = 4^3 = 64$ |
| $a^{\frac{m}{n}} = \sqrt[n]{a^m}$ | $8^{\frac{2}{3}} = \sqrt[3]{8^2} = \sqrt[3]{64} = 4$ |
| $\sqrt{ab} = \sqrt{a} \times \sqrt{b}$ | $\sqrt{16 \times 4} = \sqrt{16} \times \sqrt{4} = 4 \times 2 = 8$ |
| $\sqrt{\dfrac{a}{b}} = \dfrac{\sqrt{a}}{\sqrt{b}}$ | $\sqrt{\dfrac{16}{4}} = \dfrac{\sqrt{16}}{\sqrt{4}} = \dfrac{4}{2} = 2$ |

## ORDER OF OPERATIONS

**PEMDAS**: (Parenthesis, Exponents, Multiplication and Division, Addition and Subtraction)

Ex:

$$5 \times (4 + 5) + 2^3 - 4 \div 2$$
$$5 \times (9) + 8 - 2$$
$$45 + 8 - 2$$
$$51$$

| Algebra Review | | |
|---|---|---|
| **Name** | **Definition** | **Examples** |
| **Variable** | represents number that is unknown | $x, y, a$ |
| **Algebraic expression** | a mathematical "phrase" containing numbers, variables, and operations | $2x + 5$ |
| **Terms** | variables and/or numbers multiplied together | $17, 2x, y$ |
| **Coefficient** | number before a variable | In $9x$, the coefficient is "9" |
| **Monomial** | an expression with one term | $2x$ |
| **Binomial** | an expression with two terms | $2x + y$ |

| | | |
|---|---|---|
| **Polynomial** | an expression with more than one term | $2x + y$; $3y + 4z + 12x$ |
| **Like terms** | expressions with the same variables raised to the same power; can be combined with $+$ and $-$ in expressions | $3x + 4x + x^2 = 7x + x^2$ |
| **Distributive property** | $a(b + c) = ab + ac$ | $3x(x + 4) = 3x^2 + 12x$ |
| **FOIL method** | $(a + b)(c + d) =$ $ac + ad + bc + bd$ | $(x + 3)(x + 2)$ $x^2 + 2x + 3x + 6$ $x^2 + 5x + 6$ |
| **Factoring** | opposite of distribution; finding the greatest common factor all terms have in common | $6x^2 + 4x = 2x(3x + 2)$ $x^2 + 7x + 10 = (x + 5)(x + 2)$ $2y^2 - 11y + 12 = (y - 4)(2y - 3)$ |
| **Algebraic equation** | tells you two expressions are equal to each other | $9x = 36$ |
| **Inequality** | a mathematical statement comparing two unequal quantities | $4x + 7 < 15$ |
| **Solving inequalities** | you can preserve the inequality while solving as a normal equation, EXCEPT when multiplying or dividing by a negative number, which reverses the inequality | $5 > 3$ $5 \times (-4) < 3 \times (-4)$ $-20 < -12$ |

| Inequality Symbols | |
|---|---|
| $>$ | greater than |
| $<$ | less than |
| $\geq$ | greater than or equal to |
| $\leq$ | less than or equal to |

*For more information, refer to the Ivy Global SSAT Math Guide (see pages 133-180).*

# Geometry Review

## Lines

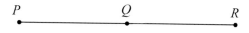

P and R are the **endpoints.**
Q is the midpoint.

## Angles

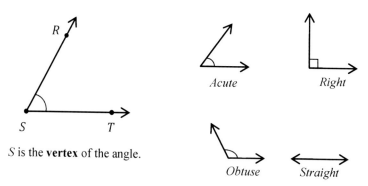

*S* is the **vertex** of the angle.

Two angles that have equal measures are called **congruent**.
A line that **bisects** an angle divides it into two equal parts.

## Transversals

Transversals intersect parallel lines.

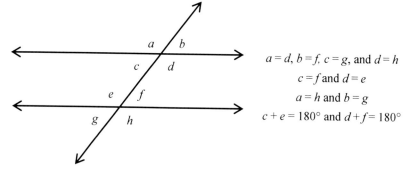

$a = d$, $b = f$, $c = g$, and $d = h$

$c = f$ and $d = e$

$a = h$ and $b = g$

$c + e = 180°$ and $d + f = 180°$

## Polygons

- The **perimeter** of any polygon is the sum of the length of its sides.
- **Congruent** polygons: have the same size and shape.
- **Similar** polygons: have the same shape, but not the same size.

## Triangles

Angles of a Triangle

The sum of the interior angles of a triangle is 180°

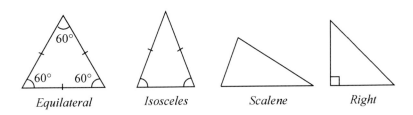

*Equilateral*  *Isosceles*  *Scalene*  *Right*

*Pythagorean Theorem* (for right triangles):

$$a^2 + b^2 = c^2$$

## Quadrilaterals

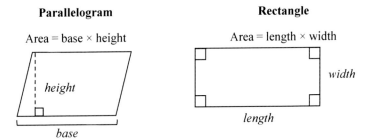

**Parallelogram**

Area = base × height

**Rectangle**

Area = length × width

20

*Ivy Global*

|                  |                  |
|:----------------:|:----------------:|
| **Square**       | **Trapezoid**    |

Area = side$^2$

$$Area = \frac{1}{2} \times height \times (base\ 1 + base\ 2)$$

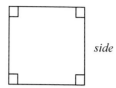

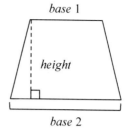

## CIRCLES

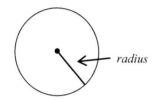

$$Diameter = 2 \times radius$$
$$Circumference = \pi d \text{ or } 2\pi r$$
$$Area = \pi r^2$$
$$Circle = 360°$$

## SOLID GEOMETRY

### Prisms

- Surface area = sum of the areas of all faces
- Volume = length × width × height

### Cylinders

- Surface area = (area of both bases) + (circumference × height)
- *Volume* = $\pi \times r^2 \times height$

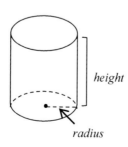

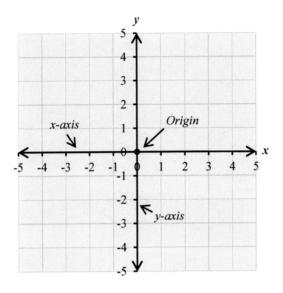

Ordered pair: $(x, y)$

Quadrants

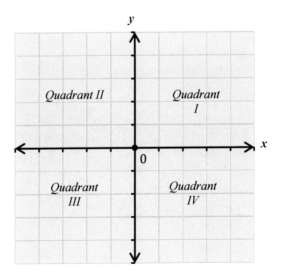

*For more information, refer to the Ivy Global SSAT Math Guide (see pages 181-256).*

# DATA INTERPRETATION REVIEW

## Bar Graphs

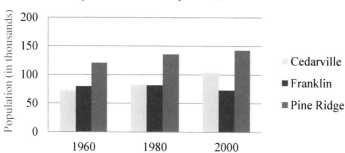

Population Growth by Town, 1960-2000

## Line Graphs

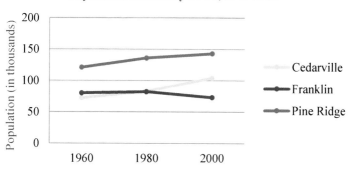

Population Growth by Town, 1960-2000

## Pie Charts

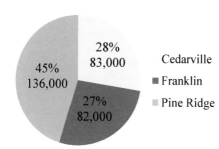

Population Breakdown by Town in 1980

| Data and Probability | | |
|---|---|---|
| Name | Definitions | Example |
| **Range** | difference between the biggest and smallest values | In 1, 3, 5, 7, the range is 6 |
| **Mean (Average)** | sum of data ÷ total number of values | In 1, 3, 5, 7, mean is 4 |
| **Median** | value that is exactly in the middle of a set of data (or, the avg. of the 2 numbers closest to the middle) | In 1, 4, 6, 11, median is 5 |
| **Mode** | the value that occurs most frequently | In 1, 1, 3, 5, mode is 1 |
| **Probability** | number of ways to get a favorable outcome ÷ number of possible outcomes | The probability of a penny landing on "heads" when flipped is 1:2 |
| **Probability of Zero** | event is impossible | The probability that a six-sided number cube will roll a number greater than 6 |
| **Probability of One** | event is certain to happen; probability cannot be greater than one | The probability that a six-sided number cube will roll a number between 1 and 6 |
| **Mutually exclusive events** | impossible for both events to happen at the same time; can find the chance of one OR the other by adding their probabilities | What is the probability of rolling either the number 5 or the number 3 on a six-sided number cube, with numbers 1 through 6? |
| **Independent events** | events may happen at the same time, but first event does not affect probability of the second; can find the chances of BOTH occurring by multiplying together their probabilities | What is the probability of rolling two even numbers on one roll of two six-sided number cubes? |
| **Dependent events** | one event affects the probability of the other occurring; can find chances of BOTH occurring by determining how the probability of the second is affected by the first and then multiplying their probabilities | Janice picked cards randomly from a standard 52-card deck. She picked her first card and then set it aside, without replacing it, before drawing her second card. What is the probability that both cards were kings? |
| **Probability and geometry** | Probability of something happening in a region = Area of specific region ÷ Area of whole figure | Probability of event in blue = Area of blue / Area of white |

## PROBABILITY EXAMPLE

What is the probability of rolling two even numbers on one roll of two six-sided number cubes, with faces numbered 1 through 6?

| 1 and 1 | 1 and 2 | 1 and 3 | 1 and 4 | 1 and 5 | 1 and 6 |
|---------|---------|---------|---------|---------|---------|
| 2 and 1 | 2 and 2 | 2 and 3 | 2 and 4 | 2 and 5 | 2 and 6 |
| 3 and 1 | 3 and 2 | 3 and 3 | 3 and 4 | 3 and 5 | 3 and 6 |
| 4 and 1 | 4 and 2 | 4 and 3 | 4 and 4 | 4 and 5 | 4 and 6 |
| 5 and 1 | 5 and 2 | 5 and 3 | 5 and 4 | 5 and 5 | 5 and 6 |
| 6 and 1 | 6 and 2 | 6 and 3 | 6 and 4 | 6 and 5 | 6 and 6 |

For each number cube, there are six possible outcomes. Our favorable outcome is rolling an even number: 2, 4, or 6. To find the probability of rolling an even number, we divide the number of favorable outcomes (3) by the number of possible outcomes (6):

$$\frac{3}{6} = \frac{1}{2}$$

The probability of rolling an even number is $\frac{1}{2}$. To find the probability of rolling an even number twice, multiply the chance of the first cube being even by the chance of the second cube being even:

$$\frac{1}{2} \times \frac{1}{2} = \frac{1}{4}$$

## PROBABILITY EXAMPLE 2

Christy has two scarves and three hats. She wants to pick one scarf and one hat to wear. How many different combinations of one scarf and one hat could she pick?

2 scarves × 3 hats = 6 possibilities

*For more information, refer to the Ivy Global SSAT Math Guide (see pages 257-286).*

# Preparing For Your Test Day

It is natural to be nervous leading up to your exam. However, if that feeling starts to become overwhelming, here are some strategies that you can use:

1. Relax and slow down.
2. Break your studying into manageable chunks.
3. Sleep and fuel up.
4. Take a break!

The night before the test:

- **Study only lightly**. Don't try to learn anything new.
- Pick out what you are going to wear to the exam—try wearing layers in case the exam room is hotter or colder than you expect.
- Organize everything you need to bring, including your **Admissions Ticket**.
- **Know where the test center is located** and how long it will take to get there.
- Have a nutritious meal and **get plenty of sleep**!

On the morning of the exam:

- Let your adrenaline kick in naturally.
- Eat a good breakfast and stay hydrated; your body needs fuel to endure the test.
- Bring along several pencils and a good eraser.
- Listen carefully to the test proctor's instructions and let the proctor know if you are left-handed so you can sit in an appropriate desk.
- Take a deep breath and remember: you are smart and accomplished! Believe in yourself and you will do just fine.

Made in the USA
Middletown, DE
11 October 2020

21389158R00015